Broken Little Pieces

K.C. Laurie

Copyright © 2024 K.C. Laurie
All rights reserved
First Edition

Fulton Books
Meadville, PA

Published by Fulton Books 2024

ISBN 979-8-89427-482-9 (paperback)
ISBN 979-8-89427-483-6 (digital)

Printed in the United States of America

Contents

Knife-Wielding Supporters and Knights
in Shining Armor 1
    Lily 3
    Blind 4
    Beautiful People Do Still Exist—and
        You Are Proof 6
    Floor 7
    Half 9
    Superhero 13
Falling Fast and Face-First 15
    Touch 17
    The Simplest Flower in the Garden 19
    Fairy Tales 21
    A Nice Way to Put It 22
    Sunshine 23
    Watch 24
    Somewhere Only Us 25
    The Sun and I 26
    25 28
The Female Experience 35
    Simple 37
    Wither 38
    One of a Kind 39
    Warm and Alone 41

Enthralled in Heartbreak 49
    Sweet but It Burns 51
    Edit Down 52
    I Hope 54
    Clean 56
    Fast 58
    Take It with You 60
    The Way You Left 61
    About the Author 70

Knife-Wielding Supporters and Knights in Shining Armor

Friends, family, and everything in between.

Lily

Her skin sat normally on her face. She was plain. No one looked at her twice; sometimes they looked for a moment longer than usual. But never twice. Unless they were together. When she walked into the room, if Lily was next to her, people stared. They could not take their eyes off Lily. Lily was the type of beautiful that made you immediately insecure. You felt like you had to bow to this beauty. And everyone knew it. But Lily did not realize how much her partner in crime hated herself. She was unaware how much her beauty killed her friend. But standing next to Lily was hard. Heartbreaking. It was clear when people catcalled them or even just looked twice on the street, it was Lily they were looking at.

Blind

It's crazy what you'll do for a friend
We will abandon ourselves for those close to us
For people who would not give you the time of day
We give our hearts to those that just add it
to a collection of other discarded items.
How are you to know that
someone will only use you?
Trust is an uphill battle that never comes down.
It is a balloon floating away into nothing.
Even then, however, all we can do is trust.
If we never believed anyone, we'd never
learn about the masks that people wear
Or the lies people tell
Or the secrets people bury
So we believe. Blindly
Until we are given our sight back.
When will I get to stay blind?

*****

Made in Your Image

She's your piece of artwork.
Every dark streak and cut.
All the imperfections mirror your own
How could you despise something
made in your image?
Is it her you detest?
Or is it you?
Do you hate yourself so much, you cannot love her?
Your blood and hers all the same
Blood isn't always thicker than water, I suppose

Beautiful People Do Still Exist—and You Are Proof

There are physically beautiful people surrounding us every day
We are suffocated with plastic beauty
However, every once in a while, someone like her comes along.
Someone whose smile lights up a room
And whose heart shines out of their eyes
She enchanted everyone she encountered
Never was anyone able to speak an ill word on her behalf
She brought sunshine to those whose lives were dark and cloudy
And she single-handedly saved me

Floor

Pressed against the wall, she slid
down and hit the floor
Her eyes were swollen and bloodshot
Her hands felt the tile under her as he sat beside her.
Her mind was fuzzy from the alcohol,
and she could barely explain herself
He knew, though.
He understood the sudden outpour of emotion
His words, however, broke through all
of the booze, soaking her brain.
"Stand up."
"Look at yourself"
"No, you are not a mess."
"You are too pretty. Too pretty to cry over him."
"He is not worth the time you are wasting."
She got up
She looked at herself
She realizes that there are people in her corner

People who do not mind the cold
tile of a bathroom floor

*****

Sweet and twisted, just like Daddy made me.
Too bad he doesn't appreciate his own work.

Half

Everything happens for a reason.
Lily walked into my life for a reason
She woke me up from a state of
simply going with the flow
I always feared if she was gone,
I'd just be half a person
I trained myself to be her other half
I ate half of meals because we shared
I bought clothes with the intention that
she would have them half the time
My heart was cut in half
Because the other half was Lily's
But then I left.
I was half a person without Lily
Short visits were not enough
When you are walking around as only
half a person every day, feels empty
My only focus was to make sure I
got back to my other half
I lived every day as just half of me
I wondered if Lily felt the same

Everything happens for a reason
And Lily was meant to be my other half

*****

If I could paint myself a new face, I would.
There is so much to change, even the things I
do not totally despise. I would change it all.
How ungrateful of me. My mother spent nine
months creating this face. Sculpting every bone, D
raining color from herself to make mine bright.
Using her body and energy to create mine.
And I would erase it all in the name of vanity.
I should be more grateful.
Thank you, Mom

*****

Hate is a four-letter word

Just a small little word

But it packs a punch when it comes flying out of the mouth that used to read you, "Once upon a time…"

I hate you.

I love you too, Dad.

It hurts to love you.
Every. Single. Second.
Burning pain that lingers for a while.
It's nice to have a friend.
Not when they're the ones holding the knife.
I'm begging you to love me.
Why can't you hear me?
I've never been so loud.

*****

Beautiful and full of magic
A fairy in the field of dragonflies and moths
Raising a different sort of fairy
She, a fairy of nature and all things lovely
Her spawn a fairy shadowed by darkness
Both wild
Both free
But only to one another.

*****

A princess is just a girl born with luck
I was never a princess
You pretended it was luck, to pull the wool over my eyes
But I am the girl with the curse

A dark cloud looms over me.
Damned from the start.
Isn't that right, Dad?

*****

Fire burns. Angry, red-hot fire.
It singes her edges, and she cracks a smile.
Chaos consumes her, and she revels in it.
Get too close, and it will swallow you too.
Dare to try?

Superhero

Daddy is supposed to be a superhero
He is supposed to be strong
And smart
And loyal
And protective
Emphasis on *supposed to*
Daddy is not supposed to be the beginning
of every issue with every man
He is not supposed to make you
feel worse about yourself
Or give you trust issues
Or lie to you
Or leave
As a child, you are supposed to be happy
You are supposed to be carefree
And fun
And young
And innocent
Children are not supposed to be responsible for
maintaining their relationship with their parent
They are not supposed to be the bigger person
Or anxious
Or stressed

Or lonely
So why is it that more often than not,
that Daddy is not the superhero?
But the child is expected to be?
There is only so much little hands can hold.

Falling Fast and Face-First

Self-explanatory.

Touch

There was something about the way you touched me. When you slid your fingertips between mine, it was like I was on fire. My head spun. When you put your hands on me, it was like I had been sleeping forever and I was waking up. Warm and safe. You slipped your fingers into the belt loops of my jeans, and I felt like they were meant to stay there. You put your hand on my cheek, and all the color drained from the rest of the world. Everything was black and white, but you and I were vibrant with color. Wrapped in your arms, I was no longer afraid. The world slipped away. The waves crashed behind us and the wind blew, but I did not hear or feel it. All that was there was you. Your touch sent me somewhere that I now long to return to. Gentle yet overwhelmingly consuming. I was like an addict; once you touched me one time, I needed more. The minutes felt like seconds, and time was slipping away from me too quickly. I think about it now, and wonder if I will ever feel it again.

It was something in the way you touched me.

The brain perceives touch through many different places. The sensory inputs rush through our whole bodies. The neurotransmitters ignite when something touches our body. You sent my neurons into shock. A touch so powerful. So meaningful. Dare I say epic.

The nighttime air was cool and a little damp. My hair had fallen limp, and my face hurt from smiling at you. I played coy. I acted as if I had no idea if you were going to kiss me. But you held your hand out, and my body reacted. I had no control. A force inside of you pulled me in. I touched your fingers with the tips of my own. I placed my palm into yours.

You folded your hand over mine, and my stomach turned. Butterflies. Those damn butterflies. You put your hand that was not holding mine onto my cheek. Ran your thumb across my face and pulled me in. My other hand quickly slid up to your chest and to the back of your head. You kissed me so softly, yet with a passion that I never understood before. The match had been lit. But then you threw gentle to the wind, and it became a wildfire. You dropped my hand and touched my thigh. I pushed into you.

I was *burning,* but I didn't care.

It was something in the way you touched me.

The Simplest Flower in the Garden

He picked her.
He did not see her for what she saw herself as.
He saw her as what she wished she was.
There was no question in his mind that she was everything.
He fell hard and fast for her.
He had no idea the things she had experienced before him.
He didn't care either.
He picked her.
He had made a mental list of the things he was looking for in a girl.
    Short
    Better personality than the last
    Golden heart
    A beautiful mess
She checked every box.
Every. Single. Box.
He thought about her every day, all day.
He did not have any worries about her being too broken.

Or too sad.
Or too complicated.
Because she was a beautiful mess.

Fairy Tales

He created a world she did not know was real. Her thighs were sore from pinching herself to be sure she was not dreaming. She lays her hands on him often to feel the warmth of his skin. "Once upon a time," they say. But what does it mean? Once in some imaginary place, a girl was beautiful, and obviously someone was to come and fall in love with her at first sight? What about the girls who were not beautiful? Not perfectly built with long hair and bright smiles. What about the girls who struggle just to fake a smile? Do those girls get a story that begins "Once upon a time"? Does their story end with "happily ever after"? She did not believe they did. She was afraid. Afraid that she would never see her prince charming simply because she did not deserve him. She had met plenty of villains. They had put on quite the show for her. Made her believe that she too was the bad guy. Then they moved on. Their story continued without her. But she was frozen in the pages. Then he picked up her story. It did not begin "Once upon a time," it just showed a girl with big blue eyes and a messy broken heart. He could've put the book back, but instead, he picked up a pen. He wrote on top of where she was trapped. It read, "Once upon a time…"

A Nice Way to Put It

I have had many pleasures in life
But none compares to knowing you.
There is nothing like the way you
immediately have made me feel safe
The person I am is not for everyone.
But you seem to not mind
I am unfamiliar with this because,
usually, one day is enough.
I am not everyone's cup of tea, as they say
Which is a nice way to say, "I'm a bitch."
But you roll with my punches
Usually, I get a good month in with someone
But then they "aren't ready for anything serious"
Which is a nice way of saying,
"I'm just not into you"
But you have been so consistent
Typically, I begin to get comfortable
But then, I'm "too good" for them
Which is a nice way of saying,
"Sorry, I just can't be a man"
But you are a man in all meanings of the word.

Sunshine

He was like a sunrise
He came out of the dark and lit up her sky
She was always the moon
Dark and curious
She only saw the light of day a few times
But then he rose as the sun
He broke through the clouds, and suddenly she was
    no longer the moon
She fell from the sky and rooted into the ground
She was no longer the moon
She gazed down at her new form
A sunflower
Reaching for his sunrise every day
Thriving from his warmth
He was a sunrise that pulled her out of the sky
She fell
Fast

Watch

I find it calming the way you look at me.
You give me peace of mind.
You know my mind wanders
But you catch it before it's too far gone.
I watch you love me
I can see it
I watch you as your body entangles mine
And I can see it
I can see how much you love me.
But it's more than that.
I can see how much I love you
The reasons I love you,
Printed right there on your face
and down your chest.
I allow myself to fall into your gaze
I do not hold back
I have fallen into the gaze of others
None of them caught me.
You did.
You caught me.
I watch you love me.
I can see it.

Somewhere Only Us

As my fingers run up your back
I am taken somewhere else.
I am taken to a place where it is only you and I.
The only feeling I ever need is the feeling of your hands wrapped around me.
The only taste my mouth craves is you.
The only thing I need to see is the look in your eyes.
The only thing I need to hear is the sound of your breath quickening.
The only scent I want is the smell of your hair as your lips slide down my neck.
It is beautiful where it is only us.
I watch as your lips meet the crease of my hip.
Your eyes meet mine.
And I can see that you, too, are taken to a place where it is only us.

The Sun and I

I watch the sun peek into the window to see your face. I don't blame it. There is peace that rests in your relaxed mouth and closed eyes. The type of peace that every morning should begin with.

I move quietly so as not to disturb you. The ends of my lips curl into a soft smile to match the ever-so-slight one you wear. As I move through the sunbeam-lit room, I find myself wanting nothing more in these moments. Me, you, and the dancing beam of sunlight that brings me back to reality.

I sit next to you, and you move into me. You intertwine yourself with me, sharing that peacefulness. It washes over me, my face softens, and I interlace my body with yours. As your chest rises and falls with every breath, my frantic, bright-pink energy softens to a glow of green.

You simplify my every move. Anxiety feels like a distant memory, long forgotten. I am childlike and lighthearted when my heart beats next to yours.

You feel like running down an empty hallway just because we can. Time has no hold, no meaning.

Bliss. It is truly blissful in your presence. I feel selfish for keeping all of you to myself. The type of comfort you offer could save lives. I know. It saved mine.

I open my eyes, slowly drawing myself from daydreams about you. I stare at you as you lay still, unbothered and cool. Again, an uncontrollable smile meets my face.

You begin to stir as I watch. Your eyes slowly open. You're staring into my imperfect face. My mind wonders why I cannot find a flaw in yours.

You are the most perfect thing I have ever had the pleasure of knowing. I do not blame the sun for now bombarding into my bedroom. It begs to see you, your face. I pray only the sun and I know of your perfection.

But I know that it is foolish of me to believe that no one else has been graced with your impeccability. I am just the lucky one. The one able to simply roll over and be reminded that it is possible to be flawless. Better yet, that the flawless can love the flawed.

25

I love you differently than I've loved anyone else.
I do not beg for you to love me in return.
I only beg that you allow me to love you.
My only want is to be able to touch you
To hold you
To look over and see you sleeping
My only need is to feel you
To have my hands run across your chest
To be welcomed into your arms by the
rise and fall of your breathing
It is different than anything I've felt before.
I do not search for validation in you.
I find peaceful attentiveness.

*****

Soft and quiet
A breeze in the summer
She never saw it
Messy and loud
A hurricane ripping through her town
That is what she saw
When would she see

Open her eyes
A beautiful sunset
Not a terrible rainstorm
He would make her see
He promised

*****

Fire ignites in his eyes. Her heart races down the road. Street signs fly by them as his mind jumps to everything but their destination. Smoke fills the space between them. She's the night. Cool and slow. Effortless and dark. He wants to see more. But all they do is drive. Down the road. Her, him, and the smoke.

*****

Fresh bar air
A playful touch
Everything moves in slow motion
If we were a movie, this would be the montage moment
Everyone can feel our love
We hide nothing
A single kiss electrifies me

The music drums on
This terrible song will always be on our soundtrack
The overplayed beat rings in my ears as the moment
   grows
You mouth the words, and I'm jealous of the lyrics
They're there on your lips
My next desired destination
Wow, I love fresh bar air

*****

The air carries me
Pushing and pulling me to you.
It's almost as if nature wants me to want you
The trees echo your soft sigh
I am at ease.
I feel you everywhere
I hope nature never falls out of love with you.
So I am encompassed in you forever

*****

Kiss me
When you're mad
Happy
Lost

Sad
Kiss me
The world is only turning for the
moment for all we know
So always kiss me

*****

A dark room.
One tiny window that the sun
never seems to pass through.
A quiet space.
No one ever visited to fill the air with life.
The soul of the room is longing.
Please break the silence.
You filled all my dark places with light

*****

Matching pajamas
Split this with me
I'll go if you do
Breakfast with a side of sex
A smile that screams everything will be okay
New things, just because we can
Ice cream at midnight

A lazily packed joint
Weed-flavored kisses
"I love you's" flying through the air
Whispers that erupt into laughter
Moments I love you most

*****

Writer's block
When you're happy, inspiration looks different.
To be short, it sucks.
What good does a happy poem do?
No one reads poetry when they're happy.
It's a fact about the genre.
But shit, I love my writer's block.

*****

Your gravitational pull matches mine
You ever so positive
Me damningly negative
No two more unalike, but well suited all the same
Your magnetized kiss is a light switch in me
Connected, and I've been awoken
Everything is clear
And everything is you.

Waves crashing and campfire embers
Mint shampoo and sandalwood aftershave
Your essence rings in my favorite things

Lingering strokes up my spine
Beautiful, debilitating chills cast frost across my ribs
My exhale singes the frost away
Passion overcomes you as the impression of your fingers draws my back into an arch
Tracing my outline, I catch a worshiping look
You crave me
And I devour that thought.

The Female Experience

Self-awareness is a beautiful curse.

Simple

She was the type of girl that saw beauty in the strangest things.

Like a broken-down home with graffiti covering the walls.

She was the type of girl that would pull you into the rain because it feels warm on her skin, and she wants you to feel the same warmth she feels.

The cool breeze of fall makes her smile.

It was the simplicity of life that gave her a reason to get out of bed.

A single red rose could change her mood.

She was the type of girl that just hearing her laugh was enough to fall in love.

She pulls you into her with a crooked smile and a childlike energy.

She believes in real love and heartfelt sentences.

She has faith that there is someone for everyone

She trusts that everything happens for a reason

Her heartbreaks were felt deep within her, but she still believes in true love

Hopelessly romantic and simply pleased.

Wither

If I could resemble a branch
Would that appease me?
Thin and lifeless
Harsh and rough
Is that what my mind begs for?
Withering away as if I were nothing
Am I satisfied now?

One of a Kind

Maybe it's me
Maybe I am the odd one out
I'm too different
An old soul
Unique
Chewed as a compliment but spat out sourly as an insult
No one wants to be different
But everyone wants to stand out
Trendsetter
One of a kind
That is digested easier and tastes just as sweet
But what is the difference?
Do I want to be an old soul?
Why do I strive to be one of a kind but cannot fathom being unique?
Maybe it would be easier if I could blend in
Uniform
Basic
Those do not sit on the tongue nicely either
Who doesn't want to be one of a kind?

*****

Being a woman
Twelve-step skincare
Ice-cold water in a mason jar
Nails tapping on a screen
Drinking juice out of the container
in your underwear
Messy buns and oversized sweatshirts
The smell of sunscreen
Taylor Swift
Aperol spritz in a big wineglass
Pink joints
Big sunglasses
These things are what make us all one
Something men will never understand
The taste of shiny lip gloss
Second-day hair
There is so much beauty in being a woman
Yet we hate everything about ourselves
But that, too, is being a woman

Warm and Alone

You shared your warmth with the world
and got nothing but icicles back.
How did you do it?
You did nothing but love, and you
got nothing but distaste back.
How did it make you feel?
You are perfect, yet you've been
assigned so many flaws
How far will you go to fix them?
You give your last breath, and they let you die
Do they regret it?
You see, I would rather be warm and alone
Than frozen with company
Because one day they will miss your warmth
Your love
Your perfection
You
And then they, too, will be full
of what they gave you
Icicles
Distaste
Flaws
Death

They'll wonder
How did you do it?
How did it make you feel?
How far will you go to fix it?
Do you regret it?
But you see, if they could only
Share their warmth
Do nothing but love
Be perfectly imperfect
Share their life
They would understand that
You chose to be warm and alone
Than frozen in their company

*****

What is a reflection?
A spiteful bitch
A liar.
People whisper, "You're beautiful"
Your reflection screams louder, "You're ugly"
Who is telling the lie?
Your mind?
Is she the spiteful bitch?
The liar

A dysmorphic hole.
It's your fault.
Stop blaming your reflection.
You spiteful bitch
A letter to envy

*****

If you could change it, would you?
Go back and love her better.
If he changed it, who would she be?
She was made of broken promises.
What would she be if he was different?
Would she like the girl?
A girl made whole and with love.
Not her current foundation of misuse and hurt.
Maybe she likes herself better damaged.
If you could change it, you wouldn't.

*****

I don't want to tell you
But the darkness is back.
You will adopt the burden
It isn't yours to bear

So I will face the darkness alone
And say nothing

*****

It is selfish to want to be prettier
You look terrible today, are you sick?
Don't wish to be thin.
Have you tried this diet?
Be low-maintenance.
Why don't you ever wear makeup?
You are perfect how you are.
You're ugly.
Getting ready should be fun.
Why are you trying so hard?
If you can never win anyway, learn to love to lose.
Be you.

*****

"I'd like to donate this," as a box slaps the counter.

"It's all the parts of me everyone said someone would love one day. I decided to give them away to whomever would like them. I never found a use for them."

The box contains:
Stomach
Thighs
Upper arms
Teeth
Laugh
Nose

The woman walked away, glad to be rid of her extra baggage. She wondered why she wasn't happier.

The donations she made were all taken. All to smiling women who had missing parts themselves. They all said the same thing.

"I had one of these years ago, I never knew how much I would miss it."

*****

I hate pretty people.
I'd wear her face if I could.
So I could hate myself too.
Well, more than I already do.

*****

In pieces, the shattered glass reflects her flaws.
Magnified and sharp.

She bleeds as she tries to erase everything
The glass spreads out, and she feels lighter
Finally, she thought. All she wanted was to be smaller.
She was too busy feeling relief to notice she disappeared.
Into just broken glass.

*****

She lives in her own world in her head
No sunshine or fields of flowers
It's an empty pit. A grave without the coffin.
She sits in the bottom, watching her life pass
In shadows and odd angles
There was a time when she clawed the dirt walls
Begging to be free, to rejoin her life
Now she takes the glimpse of joy and pretends
Plays it back in her mind

*****

Bite me
Pretty girls smile
Pretty girls are not whores
Bite me
Flesh is coated in sin

Dripping from her lips with false sweetness
Bite. Me.
No one touches the modest one
Whose sin is wasted time and youth
Bite. Me.
Pretty girls bite
And sin
And refuse

*****

Your only virtue is your "fuck it" attitude
Always be coated in salt; flies love sugar
Flies also love shit.

*****

Thorns protect her from the pain
Only she stands alone
Red rose in a garden long forgotten
The last one fighting for the sunrise
Unknowingly, she begins to fade
Refusing to stop fighting and succumb
Endings are not always happy

*****

Subtract more
Make me less
One day, I will be smaller
Take it all away
Then I'll be perfect
When I'm smaller. Less

Enthralled in Heartbreak

Hearts break around here often.

Sweet but It Burns

He never kissed her in the light of day.
He only met her lips at dusk
She never told him,
His kisses were sweet but held a touch of fire.
Fire that ignited her whole body
But left her cold when the day broke.
His kisses were sweet
But they burned all at once.

Edit Down

When you write something, they always say to edit it down.
Trim the fat
But why do we not adopt this mentality in our relationships?
They both have words
Some true
Some untrue
Writing and relationships have several similarities
So why is it that when we write, we can trim the fat
But in our relationships, we want to keep every last detail
Every fight
Every lie
Every disappointment
Every outsider inserting themselves
Edit it down
Trim away the extra
Focus on the main story
The plot
Some of the best pieces of short literature probably began as pages upon pages of words

But the writer knew that it was not all necessary to
    get the point across
Edit it down
Trim the fat

I Hope

I hope it fills the void
I hope that being surrounded by the skin of others
    replaces being surrounded by love
That you smile every day because you are now free
I hope you are happy
But I also hope
That you can't listen to that song in the car because
    you miss the sound of my voice
That you can't see the planet Saturn because you
    know that I used to love you there and back
I hope that when you wake up, you reach for your
    phone and miss my name on the screen
I hope you are happy
But I also hope
That every day, you remember the lies you spun
The hurt you caused
I hope that you know, I was never a perfect person,
    but for you, I tried
Trying was not enough for you
Trying only made you resent me
I hope you are happy
But I also hope

I hope that everything you love is tainted with bits of me
Because I was everything you wanted
Everything you needed
But you wanted to be happier
I hope you are happy
But I also hope
That she realizes, it was you, not her
That she does not believe for a second that she is the only one
I hope that she keeps her walls up
That she does not let you win
I hope you are happy
But I also hope
That you heal
That you grow
That one day you become the man I saw you to be
That the person you were the day you left me disappears
That he is replaced with the person I fell in love with
Because you are not him
You are only a fraction of that man
I hope you are happy

Clean

I watch the water run down the drain. It has a hint of salt in it as it runs down my face and blends with the tears pouring out of my eyes. I stare into the drain and watch everything you said to me wash away. All of the "I love you's" and empty promises drowning, the way I drowned in the words when they were spoken. I sit here for a while, rinsing you away.

I hate that you have touched the skin that someone else will deserve more than you. I feel like I can't get clean enough. I want to scrub away all the lies and late nights. There is not enough soap to erase the amount of times I believed a lie you told me. I am crying not for the loss of you, but for the time I wasted believing you. You don't deserve for me to waste a single second upset over you. But I owe it to myself to be angry for wasting my time. To be furious that I allowed myself to be in the same situation. I took the same wrong turn I've taken time and time again, but the only difference is this street sign says, "Right way."

I watch the water run down the drain as I begin to be finally clean from the mess that you left.

*****

Would it please you?
If I gave you what you asked?
Even if I told you it would kill me?
Of course, you say yes.
No hesitation
I've always been dead to you.
A body-holding space just for you.
I guess if it's what you want…

Here lies the girl who died for him. Nameless, he didn't know it; he never asked.

Fast

She moved quickly.
Before she knew it, her skin
bare, and his hands on it
She rushed.
Before she knew it, her phone stopped
lighting up with his name
She fell.
Before she knew it, she was begging for his attention
She pretends.
Before she knew it, she was making excuses for him
She smiles.
Before she knew it, her pillow was soaked with tears.
She lied.
Before she knew it, everyone thought she ended it
She broke.
Before she knew it, his hands touched
another girl's bare skin
She moved quickly.
Before she knew it, she gave herself to someone else
She hated it.

Before she knew it, she was just one of those girls everyone whispered about
She cried.
Before she knew it, she was alone, unless she was naked

Take It with You

When you go
Take it with you
Do not leave the mess here
Take the lies
The silence
The heartache
Take it with you
You would never leave garbage in the middle of someone's floor
So take yours with you
You already left enough of a mess to clean up
Take the rest with you
I am already half the person I was
I am exhausted from all the cleaning and the fixing
So do me a favor
Take it with you

The Way You Left

At least you left me the way you found me. They always say to put things back the way you found them, out of respect. Which you did.

When you found me, I was a mess.

Broken and messy.

I believe that maybe, just maybe, you were just trying to be respectful and leave things the way you left them.

Now do not get me wrong, I was not this way while you had me. I was a better version of myself. But I made myself that way for *you*. I did not want to be all tape and glue when I was with you. So I hid those things away. Somehow, you were convinced that the broken parts of me were fixed by something you were doing. And maybe I thought so too.

But standing here, cleaning up after the mess you left, I realize I did that. I made myself better, and I did, in fact, do so for you, but I do not need you to be better.

Only problem now is that I have to repair the damage you left.

You kissed my scars before and told me that they would go away. Now you have reopened them and added more.

It was kind of you to leave me the way you left me, however, because now I know how to begin to fix myself, considering I have been here before.

*****

How could I?
How could I bend to you?
Kneeling before you
At your will
How could you?
How could you allow me to beg?
The sun so far above me
Controlling my growth
I, a weed in the garden
You hiding behind visions of clouds
Not allowing me to ever escape being a weed
How could I?
A dandelion. Pretty for a nuisance
Mistaken for a flower
How could you?
Keep the rain from coming and washing over me
I shouldn't even ask

For you are the sun
And I, a dandelion, a fake flower

*****

>Do you hear that?
>I'm screaming for you
>Do you see this?
>I've laid my heart in my hand
>Will you touch me?
>I'm trying to be soft like her
>Does it taste good?
>I wish you'd kiss me, not her
>Do you like the smell?
>All I can smell is her
>My senses want you
>Yours long for another.

*****

"Please don't" sounded like yes to you
"Go away" was begging for you
"I want to go home" meant I will stay
Am I hearing something else?
Is what I'm saying coming out wrong?
It doesn't matter now, I suppose

You are already done.
If my answer never mattered, why did you ask.

*****

She needed more,
But only because she gave everything away.
To him.
The one who made her ugly.
How could she ask for more?
She was a puzzle, missing most of the pieces.
Never to be complete
Left in the closet after he moved out.
For the next person to throw away.
He couldn't even be bothered to do that.
She never even crossed his mind
Even with the pieces of her he took
He gave those away too.

*****

Do you like it? I made everything perfect for you.
I smiled and put my bloody hands behind my back.
So he doesn't see what it costs me.
"Yeah, it's fine."
Is it just fine?

I've ruined myself in the name of
perfection for you, and it's just fine.

*****

Was she sweeter than I?
Tossed in sugar.
Rather than the bitterness in my kiss
Seasoned with your dishonesty
Don't worry
She will sour soon
Once she is invaded by you completely
Your fungus, warping her
She'll join me among the mushrooms
And you will move on to something
once again, sweet
Something candy-coated

*****

His kiss touched deep within her
Places she longed for someone to reach
Or so she thought.
He was just stealing her body

His words meant something whimsical that she believed were drawn from her dreams
But he was manipulating her mind

His presence became her source of comfort
She felt like they were connected
He was taking her soul.

Her longing, believing, and feeling were his favorite weapons.
All she was to him was a body to have, a mind to manipulate, a soul to take.

*****

Desire ate her alive
Feigning for even a crumb of affection
She wasted away
Craving and yearning
Starving for a shred of him
Something she would unknowingly never obtain
Always just out of reach
Until all that was left was her yearning ghost
Haunting him, while he still lived oblivious.

*****

Demise is mine to succumb to
I quiver in your shadow
Unapologetically, you inhale me
My entirety is a single breath to you
Gone as quick as I came
But yet the pleasure of the moment devours my soul
Demise was all mine to behold
Still, as you exhaled me back into space
I'm the luckiest breeze on a summer day
Ignorant to my unexistence.

*****

Lying below you does not serve me anymore
I'm clawing at your sides
Fighting my way out
Except I am not
You've rendered me useless. Lifeless.
My brain rips skin from your arms
My body is still.
Good girls don't take drinks from strangers

*****

Ivy covers the part of her brain that controls logic
Invasive and quick, he overtakes her

Slinking his grasp between the pieces of her
Until he is all that is left of her
Of course, then he leaves.
Empty space remains where once
there was a girl who liked a boy.

About the Author

K.C. Laurie is a new young adult author from Middletown, Rhode Island. She draws her inspiration from personal experiences as well as the experiences of those around her. She chooses to spend her time mostly with her husband and cat. These poems are a true reflection of the inner workings of her mind, and sharing them with the world is the greatest pleasure she could have.